D1037104

Deeper Walk

A Relevant Devotional Series

VOLUME 2

GOD OF MERCY,
GOD OF RELATIONSHIP

edited by
Winn Collier

Published by Relevant Books
A division of Relevant Media Group, Inc.

www.relevantbooks.com
www.relevantmediagroup.com

© 2003 by Relevant Media Group, Inc.

Design by Relevant Solutions
Bobby Jones, Raul Justiniano, Daniel Ariza, Greg Lutze
www.relevant-solutions.com

Relevant Books is a registered trademark of Relevant Media Group, Inc.,
and is registered in the U.S. Patent and Trademark Office.

ALL RIGHTS RESERVED
No part of this publication may be reproduced, stored in a retrieval system, or transmitted, in any form or by any means—
electronic, mechanical, photocopying, recording, or otherwise—without prior written permission.

Unless otherwise noted, Scripture quotations are taken from the HOLY BIBLE, NEW INTERNATIONAL VERSION®.
NIV®. Copyright © 1973, 1978, 1984 by International Bible Society. Used by permission of Zondervan Publishing House.
All rights reserved.

Scripture quotations marked (NASB) are taken from NEW AMERICAN STANDARD BIBLE ®
(NASB) © 1960, 1977, 1995 by the Lockman Foundation. Used by permission.

Scripture quotations marked (TLB) are taken from The Living Bible: Paraphrased by Kenneth Taylor.
Copyright © 1971 by Tyndale House Publishers.

Scripture quotations marked (MES) are taken from The Message by Eugene H. Peterson,
Copyright © 1993, 1994, 1995, 1996, 2000. Used by permission of NavPress Publishing Group. All rights reserved.

Scripture quotations marked (AMP) are taken from The Amplified Bible.
The Old Testament copyright © 1965 by The Zondervan Corporation. The Amplified New Testament,
copyright © 1954, 1958, 1987 by the Lockman Foundation. Used by permission.

Library of Congress Control Number: 2002094144
International Standard Book Number: 0-9714576-6-2

For information:
RELEVANT MEDIA GROUP, INC.
POST OFFICE BOX 951127
LAKE MARY, FL 32795
407-333-7152

03 04 05 06 9 8 7 6 5 4 3 2 1

Printed in the United States of America

Deeper Walk

A Relevant Devotional Series

VOLUME 2

GOD OF MERCY,
GOD OF RELATIONSHIP

edited by
Winn Collier

CONTENTS

Preface   vii

GOD OF MERCY

1   Who are the Tax Collectors?   2
2   Whitewashed Tombs   4
3   Wearing God's Pants   6
4   The Dart of Cynicism   8
5   Randy's Rules   10
6   God is Relevant   12

IN DEPTH | Getting Out of the Faith Ghetto   15

7   Forgive These People   20
8   Escaping the Comparison Trap   22
9   A Spirit of Prostitution   24
10   A Modern Day Prodigal   26

IN DEPTH | Christianity Is for Losers   29

GOD OF RELATIONSHIP

CONTENTS

1 The Silence of the Song   36
2 The Right Tool   38
3 Obedience   40
4 In Search Of   42
5 Holding God's Hand   44
6 Warm Embrace   46
7 Goodbye   48
8 Heard Above the Din   50

IN DEPTH | The Light Has Enough Light   53

9   Right or Righteous   58
10 Don't Be A Square   60
11 Straight Ahead   62
12 Tandem Jump   64
13 Name Builder   66
14 A Perilous Safety   68
15 Sound   70
16 A Holy Tasting   72
17 Seeing Grace   74
18 Disciple-Making Sandwich   76
19 If It Ain't Broke, Don't Fix It   78

Author Index   81

PREFACE

We have lost what it means to live. Thus we have lost what it means to die.

In *Working the Angles*, Eugene Peterson laments the loss of the day "when pastoral work was defined as preparing people for a good death." There seems to be little demand for this type of pastoral vocation. It's a shame because eternity waits on the other side of the hearse.

We hear a haunting whisper in our hearts that life is more than a portfolio, a title, or a pristine spiritual image. It has become cliché to acknowledge our need for a slower pace, a more reflective encounter with the world and people around us. Yet seldom does this cliché translate to an *actual* slower pace. And the art of reflection, for most of us, is like Shakespeare: we all agree he's good, but *read* him? Few of us actually have.

For years, those who care about our spiritual life have warned us of the peril we are inviting. Like the lonely voice of Noah, these prophets have called us to stop, to look around us, and to look at ourselves. They are convinced if we would only look … we would be terrified by what we saw. And we would listen. But we refuse to stop, and we certainly refuse to look. And so, we ignore their warnings. And the dark rain clouds hover on the horizon.

Why is this our lot? Why do we press harder and move faster, knowing all along it is killing our souls? Despite being convinced there is a desperate need to pause, why do we only press harder on the pedal?

What are we running after?

Better yet, what are we running from?

I suspect we are running from ourselves. The biggest lie we have believed is not that we need to get more, achieve more, or be more, as hideous as those are. The biggest lie we have believed is that life depends on us. We have succumbed to the ancient deception, winding all the way back to a garden, a tree, and the greatest tragedy ever told.

"God isn't good. He's holding out on you. You're on your own."

The lie was believed, and the fruit was taken. And we

have followed the elusive fruit ever since. So we can never pause long enough to look at the world we have created for ourselves because our heart knows that if life really depends on us, we are certainly doomed. And so we run.

What they needed in the garden is still all we need today: God. Yet in believing the delusion that life is found in everything *other* than God, we seal our fate. In the garden, life was never so good as the cool evening walks with the Creator. In modern life, those quiet connections with God offer the same balm, the same sense of wholeness.

After the great tragedy when God was refused and destruction unleashed, what our oldest father and mother desperately needed is *again* all we need today: mercy. Yet if we insist that life is all about us, we refuse mercy. We never see the need for it. It is simply a word, void of power, void of healing.

And at the end of our days, we have no idea how to die. Nothing we have given ourselves to has prepared us for this threshold. We have no control over what greets us on the other side. Our life has been built on us, and it is frightening to stand on the edge of our existence ... alone.

But what if life now is simply a prelude? What if the real concerto is being played in the world beyond death? What if in fact the notion of death is a misnomer, and death in this reality is simply the doorway to the next?

What if life has very little to do with you, yet everything to do with God? What if mercy were freely offered, abundant and free? What if you didn't have to earn it, and regardless of how you used it, it was offered again … and again … and again? What if God really wanted you to know Him? What if you could still walk in the cool of the afternoon with the Creator?

You can.

Whether you started your journey with God long ago and find yourself needing to be reminded of the truest things, eternal things, or whether you are just beginning to consider your spiritual life, we hope this volume of the *Deeper Walk: A Relevant Devotional Series* reminds you of a God who waits. He waits for you. He waits with arms full of mercy.

So, learn to live—truly live—and when the time comes, you will also know how to die. The realities of both the here and the hereafter flow from the wounds of a Savior who died to offer you everything you need: Himself, and the mercy only He offers, mercy necessary for this life and the next.

Winn Collier, editor

GOD
OF
MERCY

⌐WHO ARE THE TAX COLLECTORS?⌐
Jeremy Hunt

Jesus clashed against cultural norms of His time. He worked on the Sabbath, ministering to those in need. He cleansed the temple, driving the moneychangers out of His Father's house. A great portion of His time was spent simply being with people rather than seeing to the standard religious practices, and this behavior raised the eyebrows of the religious leaders. His willingness to hang out with the despised and rejected (such as tax collectors) was in stark contrast with the attitudes and actions of the Pharisees. In the their eyes, He made Himself unclean by being with these outcasts.

His behavior wouldn't be news to anyone familiar with Christianity, but it does raise an interesting question: Who were the tax collectors? In Christ's day, they were people like Matthew and Zacchaeus. These men charged local taxpayers too much in order to make extra profit for themselves. They were understandably disliked for their tactics. Yet Jesus took the time to be with them and minister to their needs. He even called Matthew to be among His close circle of disciples. How could He do such a thing? How could He accept those who lie, cheat, and steal from others? His actions cause us to pause. He loved those who were despicable and unlovable.

Reflection on His actions should prompt us to reconsider our question, slightly modified: Who are the tax collectors in our day? Who are the hated and unwanted in our society? In a time of political correctness and acceptance of everyone (at least on the surface), the answers won't be found in the mere identification of a specific social, racial, or cultural group. No, we must dig deeper to examine our hearts and see where our personal prejudices lie. The Pharisees looked down on those who they considered to be unclean and unworthy. Who do you disparage in your life? Who do you despise and reject?

We must act and extend the love of Jesus to all. This is where our faith becomes real. There may be times when our brothers and sisters in Christ don't understand our actions. But we are called to follow and imitate Jesus in all things. He wrapped His arms of mercy around the tax collectors and sacrificed Himself for them. Through His love, we can do the same.

EVEN DEEPER
Read Luke 18:9-14. Confront your prejudices. Take the love of Christ to someone you have been tempted to discard.

PRAYER
Father, You are the God of sinners, tax collectors, and harlots—basically people just like me. Allow me to see myself as one in need of grace. Then allow me to offer that grace to others who need it as desperately as I do.

⌐WHITEWASHED TOMBS⌐
Eric Hurtgen

What is the testimony of a culture that finds plastic surgery newsworthy? What is the testimony of a culture where violent teenage killers come from affluent suburbs, where lawns are perfectly manicured and each car has a perfect shine?

We know an outer sparkle isn't always an honest reflection of what's inside. Moldy bread is a signal that it is spoiled and needs to be thrown out. But how many of us know that days before the mold forms, it is already laced with mold on the inside? Eating bread then is just as dangerous as when the mold is visible. The testimony of our culture may be that it was poisoned on the inside long before we saw the result.

Jesus knew that people and cultures looking good on the outside did not always mean they were healthy on the inside. He pointed out His disgust for such hypocrisy: "Woe to you … (who) clean the outside of the cup and dish, but inside are full of greed and self-indulgence … First clean the inside of the cup and dish, and then the outside also will be clean" (Matthew 23:25-27). He called the Pharisees "whitewashed tombs," fine-looking on the exterior but inwardly full of death and decay.

What are our cleaning techniques? Have we cleaned our outsides, but let our inward selves, our souls, remain dirty and stained? For us to truly become Christ followers, we can't rely on outward conformity. That will only produce "whitewashed tombs."

EVEN DEEPER
Read and pray David's prayer in Psalm 51.

Focus on the "inside of the cup" this week. Rather than centering on those actions that fall short of the Father's holiness, meditate on the heart condition that precedes those actions.

PRAYER
Thank You, Jesus, for such surprising grace and favor! I humbly ask for more grace as I seek to let my heart be cleaned. Send Your streams of living water to flow through me. Give me patience as Your work continues in my life!

⌒WEARING GOD'S PANTS⌒
Jessica Leopold

In Luke, Jesus offered this parable: "No one tears a patch from a new garment and sews it on an old one. If he does, he will have torn the new garment, and the patch from the new will not match the old" (Luke 5:36).

The Pharisees were always looking for a fault in Jesus. This parable was in response to their concern over His association with "sinners" such as Levi and his rabble-rousing buddies. In response, Jesus tells the story about a "garment," but to better understand the verse, we could paraphrase it to say: "No one with any sense would buy a new pair of pants only to rip them apart in order to patch up an old pair of pants!"

It seems Jesus intended the old pants to represent the Old Covenant and the new pants to represent the New Covenant He was introducing. What does God's story contrasting the Old and New Covenant have to do with us? What is our responsibility to Christ's instructions about new pants?

We say we love God. We practice a spiritual discipline here and there. We pursue a few of the principles we presume promise a happy life. But in reality, these are simply surface gestures, small patches holding our tattered, saggy pants together. We have never really changed into our new pants, still hanging spotless in our closet. We have never fully embraced the new life God provides.

Each time a new hole sprouts in our old pants, we rip a small piece of fabric from the closet: a little moment of prayer or a few Scriptures. But we are denying the inevitable: the old pants will never fit.

Jesus never intended to be a "quick fix." He is not a God of extra pieces. He scraps the old stuff and makes everything new. We do not have to be trapped in a terminal cycle of brokenness and struggle without relief. Jesus died so we could live a life freed from the guilt of sin. He died to clothe us in all things new.

EVEN DEEPER
Read Romans 6:4 and 2 Corinthians 3:6. Take a look in your closet. Peer deep in the back where you seldom look. Are you still hanging on to some things you should have thrown out years ago? Now, do the same in the closet of your soul.

PRAYER
God of the New Covenant, You have set me free. I am no longer bound to old ways, old paths, or old hurts. You have released me. Strengthen me to walk in the new life You bring.

⤙THE DART OF CYNICISM⤚
Jennifer Ashley

Some sins are obvious: pride, lust, anger. Then some sins are more subtle and not often talked about, such as cynicism. God didn't write on Moses' stone tablets, "Thou shall not be cynical." No parable guards against it.

Our generation is fuming with cynics: religious cynics, political cynics. They're funny, they're paranoid, and they're celebrated. It is hip to distrust, to assume the worst, to doubt, and to question authority.

Nobody wants to worship with a bunch of show-offs or phonies. We want authenticity. But we've become so suspicious of church leadership and thriving fellowships that sometimes it's hard to do the simple things: to trust and obey and to worship God with all our heart, mind, soul, and strength.

And cynicism spreads. First you start to doubt the motives of a pastor: Does he want us to be giving with our time so his own programs will succeed? Then you wonder about the authenticity of those around you: Are they trying to look spiritual to get attention? Satan is so tricky.

For years, I was a cynic. I didn't realize the damage it was doing. In my college fellowship I was never able to worship freely because I was always suspicious, focusing on the motives of the people around me instead of focusing on Christ. For years, I didn't tell my friends of the amazing forgiveness I had received. I was surrounded by lonely, restless people, but I didn't share my story with them. I didn't think they *genuinely* wanted it. I was a cynic.

Eventually they started saying, "I want to know. I want to read the Bible. I want to come to church." I was shocked. Years later, I grew more aware of the spectacular attractiveness of our holy God. He offers what no one else can and what everyone wants: meaning, purpose, passion, and boundless love.

Cynicism is an easy mask to wear, but it will blind you to the call of Christ and blind you to the heart of others.

EVEN DEEPER
Read Hebrews 10:22. List five comedians, musicians, or political figures who have influenced you to be cynical. How has each conditioned you to distrust love, leadership, religion, and sincerity? Think about how this might affect your relationship with God and your spiritual community.

PRAYER
God, forgive me for doubting the power of Your truth. Strip away the cynicism in my heart and allow me to enjoy a full life of worshipping You.

⮞RANDY'S RULES⮜
Kent D. Curry

I often take Caleb, my rambunctious three year old, to a nearby park so he can burn off some energy. The playground has two of these massive why-didn't-they-have-these-when-I-was-growing-up mini-gymnasiums with twisting slides, ladders, monkey bars, multi-level platforms, and sliding poles protruding out of them at mad angles.

One evening, five-year-old Randy rode up on his bike and asked Caleb to play tag. Caleb agreed. Randy announced the rules: 1. Each person got three timeouts. 2. Caleb was "it."

Randy raced off and my smaller, less nimble son began a futile quest to touch him. Naturally, Randy was never in any danger. I encouraged Caleb loudly and tried not to seethe at the gross inequities of the game. Eventually, Randy realized this wasn't much fun, so he magnanimously declared that I could assist my son. Soon we forced Randy into burning two of his timeouts.

When we cornered him into his final timeout, Randy announced that, actually, everyone got extra timeouts. When I insisted on the original rules, Caleb tagged him.

Randy then jumped on his bike and prodded Caleb to chase him. Daddy made sure Caleb didn't. After pedaling around in circles, Randy went home. Caleb wondered why he left, and I attempted to explain how Randy didn't want to play by his own rules.

I'd still be annoyed at him except for this reminder of how often I try to change the rules on God. He asks me to obey, and I enact the Stupid Rule (if I think it's stupid, I don't have to do it) or any other personal precept that makes room for my behavior.

Submission may be the toughest part of the Christian walk. Pride makes dying daily a difficult task. We often forget: "Don't you know that when you offer yourselves to someone to obey him as slaves, you are slaves to the one whom you obey—whether you are slaves to sin, which leads to death, or to obedience, which leads to righteousness?" (Romans 6:16).

The truth remains: You can't half-obey. You either obey or rebel. You prove your Christian maturity through obedience, not independence. On the playground, Randy may have made his own rules, but God rules the playground we call life.

EVEN DEEPER
Read Matthew 6:10 and 2 Timothy 2:4-6. Do you struggle with attempting to play your way with God? What God is calling You toward?

PRAYER
God, point out the places where I am insisting on my own way. Help me to embrace Your leading today.

⌐GOD IS RELEVANT⌐
Robin Lemke

A heavy leather Bible sits on a table in an antique store. Its intricate carvings are filled with dust, and the gold that once distinguished its pages is almost entirely worn off. One day, the old Bible sells for a large sum of money, and the purchaser tucks it into a bag to take home and proudly place on a lofty shelf.

Is this the place God holds in our life? Down a dark, narrow corridor between the little known and the lesser used? Is God removed from our daily cares and contemporary concerns, part of a world of camels and patriarchs, white robes, and Roman rule? We can get so carried away with putting Scripture into the context of its own day that we forget its relevance to ours.

Jesus came to the common people and spoke to their current problems. Rather than offering long-winded treatises on Levitical law, he summed up the commandments with: Love God and love each other. He outwitted the scholars and enlightened the masses with the same words. Christ came to be active, pertinent, and powerful, not to dust off scrolls and weigh down His people with rules. He came to save us. He said, "My yoke is easy and my burden is light" (Matthew 11:30). Jesus understood the weight the people carried, and He took it on Himself.

Today we deal with abuse in the church, a changing family unit, questions of sexual identity, racial tensions, human cloning, and suicide bombers. We may feel these concerns are too much for God, but none of it overwhelms Him. He is with us as we check on our sleeping children. He feels our fear as we make airline reservations. The facts may seem too crushing for us to grapple with, but not so for God.

Jesus said, "Have you not read what God said to you, 'I am the God of Abraham, the God of Isaac, and the God of Jacob.' He is not the God of the dead but of the living" (Matthew 22:31-32). And today He is my God and your God. He is not obscure. He is relevant.

EVEN DEEPER
Read Psalm 46:1 and Hebrews 13:8. Ponder your week. What parts of it have you been tempted to think God was disengaged from? How do you think even those parts might be part of His handiwork?

PRAYER
God, thank You for being the God of the living.

Getting Out of the Faith Ghetto
Dan Buck

If I had a video store, it would have one section: Movies. I'm not sure what effect that would have on business, but it would certainly reflect a lesson I've been learning and relearning from the moment I began thinking for myself. The lesson is this: Life is one category. It seems simple enough, and hardly earth shattering, but as I think about its implications, I find myself awe-struck by the possibilities of a life lived from this mindset.

Do you remember how the books you read in literature courses were always set in a historical context that your English professor often felt inadequate to discuss without the help of a history professor? Have you wandered aimlessly up and down the supermarket aisle designated "Sauces" looking desperately for soy sauce only to discover that it's actually kept in the "Ethnic Foods" aisle? And have you recently noticed that the most casual of conversations with a non-believer has an alienating "spiritual aspect" to it even though you were trying to avoid being too "Christiany"? The reason for all these quandaries is the same: Life is one category.

———

GOD PENCILED IN

Postmodernism has given a shot in the arm to spirituality, but unfortunately, it has been relegated to a spot in our daytimer between a stop at Starbucks and the health club. We have made God a category in our life. And we think we're improving in our walk when we spend more time in that category: "The more often I have morning devotionals, the better Christian I am." And while morning devotionals are important, the truth is your time in Revelation is as spiritual as your chat with a co-worker over the water cooler.

Psychologist Paul Tournier said we have created an image of mankind that is, in essence a list: physical, emotional, mental, and spiritual. Tournier would argue that spirituality is not on that list but at the center of the other three. It is the source of our physical, mental and emotional output and the recipient of all input through those means as well. In other words, there is no way to be solely spiritual. Go ahead, be spiritual. Ready? … One … Two … Three, go! What did you do? Trying to be spiritual away from the rest of our life is like trying to eat without any food or like trying to be a really good driver without ever going down the road. We get in and study the steering wheel and gauges, then we get out of the car and start walking down the road. It's in everyday life that our spirituality can be exercised. Our spiritual battle is fought a million times a day in a million different ways. It is in the effort we put into our work; it's in the way we talk to our loved ones; and it's in the speed with which we return our neighbors borrowed hedge trimmer.

THE CHRISTIAN GHETTO

Within the Church there is a strange effort to counteract this effect by bringing our pseudo-spiritual subculture around with us everywhere we go. We turn the world into a large church service full of people who believe like we do and who don't offend our sensibilities with their sinful behaviors. Opening a phone book, I can find Christian pharmacies, Christian art framing, Christian bakeries, and here in my hometown, someone has created a business concept out of a cheesy Christian T-shirt. The Lord's Gym Health and Fitness Centers are dedicated to promoting "Fitness for Body & Soul" and offer classes such as Praise Dance, Body of Armor and Chariots of Fire Spin.

Some might argue such businesses are a good model of stretching the barriers of our spiritual activity beyond Sunday morning. However, all they are doing is adding spiritual language into things that are naturally spiritual because they are part of the human experience God has created. Taking care of your body is spiritual even if you don't play the Newsboys while working on your biceps.

These "Christian" shops are doing what all the "secular" shops are doing, but to the exclusion of non-believers. Creating these places completely removes God's disciples from the world, which doesn't bode well for the world, and I daresay, ends up hurting the Church as well.

What's occurring is the creation of a *ghetto*. The word has long since been associated with inner city housing projects and Elvis' worst song ever, but the ghettos have been around since the Middle Ages. Then they were walled sections of a city that a religious group (usually Jews) was forced to occupy as a way of keeping it from the rest of the population. Christians appear to be doing it to themselves. And within the walls of this Christian ghetto we're not only experiencing death in the Church but in the arts as well.

Go to a Christian bookstore. As you walk the aisles you'll see shelf after shelf of Christian toys (usually of poor quality), Christian music (usually a little worse than the toys) and over on the right side, by the Christian coffee shop called "Jesus Java" you'll see a shelf labeled "Art." This shelf consists of a Thomas Kinkade painting and two photo landscapes, all with Bible verses or Oswald Chambers quotations emblazoned across the top right corner. Here we are, the group of people that claims to have the corner market on understanding the first and greatest Artist and we can't even imitate His creative nature as effectively as a world that doesn't know Him.

THE LAZY CHRISTIAN'S GUIDE TO PRUDENCE

We have categorized ourselves out of the world. Life should be one category. Good music, good art, good health and good prescription drugs are innately spiritual if they are in fact good. We don't need to label something Christian to the exclusion of the rest of the world for it to be good and pure. All things that are good and pure are of God, whether the name on it is Rich Mullins or David Gray. All truth is God's truth. If we are seeking God out in everything we do, He will show up. He doesn't need labels or categories to find us, and we shouldn't need them to find Him. Sure, some experiences you should steer clear of, but He has given us a mind, a body of believers, and the Holy Spirit to help us decipher what is of Him and what is not.

Our categories have become the lazy Christian's guide to prudence. "I don't have to worry about what messages are in this movie—it's Christian." Not only is that argument a dangerous fallacy, but it also leads to the exclusion of truth God is revealing to us through "non-Christian" sources. In God's cosmic video store there is one category: truth. It's not supposed to be easy. Every experience, every person you meet, and every choice you make is a part of the walk. It takes a lot more work and thinking on our part, but we must at least read the back of every video before determining its worth. The good news is: There are no late fees. You don't have to have all the answers. We'll have the answers someday, but for now, look for God everywhere. He might even be found in that stupid Elvis song.

⟨FORGIVE THESE PEOPLE⟩
Faith Hopler

"Father, forgive them, for they do not know what they are doing" (Luke 23:34).

Why did Jesus make this request? His sacrifice of His own life clearly demonstrated His commitment to His murderers' forgiveness. Why were these among His final words?

An old story tells of a child princess forced to flee from an enemy marching to attack her home while her father, the king, is away. An old, faithful soldier dresses in her father's robes and crown, hoping he will be mistaken for the king. He knows he will lose his life when captured, but he sees no other way to draw attention away from the princess. The child, headstrong and terrified, condemns the man, calling him a traitor as she is forcibly whisked away. The old soldier stood, watching her, and said, "These words have dropped to the ground between us; think nothing of them when the time comes."

Later the princess realized the sacrifice he made for her. She bitterly regretted her words, but she realized that he, in his graciousness, foresaw her eventual self-loathing. He not only forgave her but also provided her a way to forgive herself.

Jesus longed to forgive the arrogant sins of each who had condemned Him with their words and their silence. He knew no one understood His substitution or the weight of our sins. He knew a time would come when they would realize their helplessness and His sacrifice. Peter would crouch, weeping as the cock crowed. Some among the bloodthirsty crowd would eventually despair, knowing they had crucified the Messiah.

It was for these moments that He spoke His dying words on the cross—the moments when we, sickened by our shame, nearly reach the despair of Judas. Jesus speaks to us from the cross, telling us our sin has been forgiven, covered by His sacrifice. This is the piercing graciousness of our Lord and Savior: In the moment of His death, hanging from the cross we nailed Him to, He forgave us. And He invites us to forgive ourselves, take up His grace, and clothe ourselves at the foot of the cross.

EVEN DEEPER
Study Luke 5:32, 2 Corinthians 7:10 and Revelation 3:19. Open up the dark closet of your soul. Trace back to your deepest wounds. Is there something from your past you are holding onto, unwilling to believe that God's forgiveness can free you? Bring it to the light of the cross.

PRAYER
Forgiving Father, why do I run from you? Why do I think my sin surprises you? Not only do you know each wretched crevice of my heart, you provided for them. God, wash me in waves of forgiveness.

⸙ESCAPING THE COMPARISON TRAP⸙
Margaret Feinberg

"Follow me." Those words still echo. An invitation and a challenge. Fulfill your destiny. Be what you are called to be. Walk out your faith.

Just as our physical bodies can't take a step or even function at all unless each member is committed to its own task, the body of Christ can't function without each member fulfilling its unique role. For that reason, it's pointless to compare our purpose with another's.

Peter fell into a comparison trap after breakfast one morning. Jesus responded with a prophesy: "I tell you the truth, when you were younger you dressed yourself and went where you wanted; but when you are old you will stretch out your hands, and someone else will dress and lead you where you do not want to go" (John 21:18).

Strong words. They came from the Master, the Son of God. They're words no one would want to hear, including Peter.

Something in the young disciple wanted to turn away. There had to be a way of escape from this fate. An option. An alternative. His eyes wandered to a fellow disciple: the one whom Jesus loved. Peter couldn't help himself (he rarely could), and he questioned Jesus, "Lord, and what about him?" Jesus reply was full of love but stern, "If I want him to remain alive until I return, what is that to you?" Peter felt the sting, a reminder that not all callings are the same. Jesus concluded with a command: "Follow me!"

The journey ahead of Peter was one he alone could travel. A reminder that there is only one proper comparison in the Kingdom of God: Jesus Christ, the standard. What is He asking of you? Like Peter, it may end in death—or something that feels much like it. Will you follow? What has Christ called you to?

EVEN DEEPER
Read 1 Corinthians 12:12-31. Is there anything God has called you to that remains undone? If so, what will it take for you to be obedient?

PRAYER
Father, forgive me for comparing myself to others. Help me to recognize You as the only standard. Forgive me for any areas of disobedience. I want to obey.

⮞A SPIRIT OF PROSTITUTION⮜
Jennifer Ashley

Prostitution is not something you want in your family. You might be brave enough to mention that your sister is an exotic dancer or your girlfriend is a cocktail waitress. But no one wants to go to bed with his at night and think, "This woman has slept with half this city."

I am a prostitute. And my husband married me willingly. He picked me out of hundreds of women. He's handsome, brave, and he chose me. Even though he knew my tendency to betray him, he asked me to join him for the rest of his life.

And I have news for you: you're a prostitute, too.

Hosea was a prophet sent to show Israel its unfaithfulness to God. And God asked Hosea, a guy with an upstanding reputation, to marry a woman named Gomer—a locally known whore. Gomer continued to be unfaithful to Hosea throughout their marriage. Why would God ask Hosea to do something so humiliating? Because He wants us to be convinced He would do the same. We are Gomer. And God takes us as His bride.

He chose us, even though we repeatedly turn our backs on Him. We doubt. We hate. We're jealous. God knows the darkness in our hearts. Yet His love is brave and flawless, grand enough to engulf our past, and even our present. He wants to be married to us, a public, permanent act—a covenant.

Prostitution may not be our occupation, but we may be selling ourselves to everything but God. God's charge against Israel was their "spirit of prostitution"—their rebellion against God.

And in spirit, we have given ourselves to things, thinking they'd bring us more pleasure than God offers. We have adored, longed after, and worshipped things other than Christ. God still wants you. God longs to forgive and cleanse so you can worship with a new heart.

In Hosea, God pronounces to Israel: "I will betroth you to me forever; I will betroth you in righteousness and justice, in love and compassion. I will betroth you in faithfulness, and you will acknowledge the Lord" (Hosea 2:19-20).

It is a good thing God marries prostitutes. Otherwise, we'd be lonely, abandoned on the street, never knowing true love.

EVEN DEEPER
Make a list of your "little rebellions"—things you give yourself to, things that encourage a spirit of prostitution. How do those things leave you empty?

PRAYER
God, thank You for coming after me even though I am not worthy of Your bold love. Strip the rebellion from my heart. Help me give myself to You alone, to worship You with a pure heart.

The Gospel is for sinners. Sounds simple—a review of fourth grade Sunday school material leaping from the flannel graph. However, I sense it is time for a return to the most fundamental of Christian truths: the Gospel.

In the Gospel, we find hurting, scabbed over, sinful, self-willed, arrogant, rebellious, lonely wrecks offered hope and the very life of God. What we desperately needed, He became for us ... and in us. Few would disagree. Unfortunately, however, we normally view all this in the past tense. We look back at the Gospel. The Gospel isn't just the initial message prompting us onto the path of God's kingdom. The Gospel is what we need every moment of our existence, each baby step down the path.

Reviewing the story of the prodigal, the abrupt ending is striking. We aren't told how the elder brother responded to his father's tender request he join the celebration and surrender his bitter self-righteousness. The "dark character" in the parable's plot had been the younger son whose greed had shamed himself, his father, and his family. However, the story ends with an unanticipated turn: The younger son is broken in His Father's arms while the elder son is defiant to His Father's invitation.

The story is left hanging, and amazingly, the elder son becomes the "dark character," brooding outside the party of forgiveness. This craftily turned climax must have disturbed the Pharisees as they recognized Jesus identifying

them with the elder brother. The elder brother was disgusted with the father's affection for his wayward son, and the Pharisees would have joined that disgust.

Jesus aimed to challenge their pretentious **righteousness.** In scorning the prodigal's return, on some levels they became him. Which sin is worse? Leaving the father ... or refusing the father? Some prodigals sin "big" and then wake up from their foolishness. Some prodigals sin "little" and stand just outside the embrace of grace.

Many have been radically changed by grace. We are amazed by it ... drawn to it ... overwhelmed by it ... incredibly thankful for it. However, we may need to come to a new place: the realization that we need it. It is proper to be thankful for the heart of the gracious father in the story of the prodigal sons. In this new place, though, we see ourselves in the story: we are the prodigals. The Gospel is for prodigals. Like us.

EVEN DEEPER
Sit down with the story in Luke 15. Ask yourself which character you are. How do you need to come home?

PRAYER
Gracious Father, I have wandered from You. Sometimes I wander in open rebellion, relishing sin rather than You. God, I need the Gospel. I need it each time I see my sin, and even more when I don't. I am a prodigal. Help me to run with reckless abandon, home to You.

When I changed my e-mail address to christianityisfor-losers@hotmail.com, I found it both enjoyable and amusing to sit back and read the varied responses from friends and family. Some people were confused. "What kind of e-mail address is that? Is there a deeper meaning?" Others were offended. "Are you calling me a loser?" Some people seemed rather concerned about my spiritual condition. "Are you still a Christian? Are you backsliding?" Then there was my aunt, who said nothing but signed her next e-mail to me: "A loser, Auntie Lois."

I have to admit, I thrived on the small controversy that unfolded before me. I grinned when offended friends sent me e-mails. I quite enjoyed keeping people in the dark. "What does it mean?" they would ask. "Think about it," would be my reply. Christianity is for losers. What a stupid, irreverent statement for a Christian to make!

Or is it?

First off, can one say the opposite, that "Christianity is *not* for losers," or "Christianity is for winners?" Let's look back to the early days of Christianity. No, let's look to Christ Himself. In the Word, we are given accounts of the kind of company Jesus met with and the people He called. Who did He call? Who did He invest most of His time? With "good people"?

After all, that is what we would expect right about now. If Christ were here today, many of us would expect Him to be in the company of "good people." Many of us would look for Him right alongside Billy Graham and Matt Redman. Why shouldn't He be with them? They are good Christian folks, as am I! Of course, we all think Jesus would want to hang out with us. But who did Christ call and hang out with? A tax collector. An adulteress. A traitor. Fishermen. A coward. This group does not exactly look like an unshakeable foundation for the Kingdom of God, but as we look closer, we see that that is precisely why He chose and used them.

They were losers.

Because they were not good enough, only He could be. Their own miserable condition forced them to build on something larger and stronger than themselves. It's sad how we have fallen into the Pharisaical trap of thinking Christianity is for good people, like us. This is a myth. Christianity is not for good people; it never has been.

Somewhere, somehow we got confused into thinking Christianity is not for losers. This has had two rather large negative effects.

First of all, many people have turned away from Christ and the Church because they feel they are not good enough. They are painfully aware of their own inadequacy, and, in many cases, Christians only intensify their awareness. Thus they turn away, for they reason that they are not good enough to be Christians. What they fail to see is that "not being good enough" is the very first prerequisite to being a Christian. If you are good enough to be a Christian, then you need not become one. Indeed, you cannot. The essence of the Christian faith is that we fall short. We cannot bridge the gap—the gaping chasm between man and God. Only He can bridge it. We must realize that, and embrace it as a foundational truth in both theology and practice. Our righteousness truly is nothing more than filthy rags.

The second effect this myth has had is that it breaks down any differentiation between Christianity and other religions. If Christianity is for good people, than it is nothing more than just another religion. There is nothing to set it apart from belief systems like Hinduism and Islam. In religion, you get what you deserve. True Christian teaching stakes the radical claim that the opposite is true! The Christian does not get the punishment that he deserves, instead he receives that which he does not deserve! Christianity stands in stark contrast to all other religions because of this. Grace and karma are like black and white. However, if our Christianity is based on the myth that it is a belief system for good people, then the grace which we profess is not grace at all, but karma in disguise. It is true that Christianity is not a religion. But man has and is able to turn it into one. We must be wary of that.

When asking people what they thought my e-mail address meant, a few thought about it and said, "You must be talking about what Christianity has become, with all its rules and hypocrisy. That is for losers." No, that's backwards. Fake, religious Christianity is for win-ners—people that are good enough and have it all together. People who think that they do not need grace.

But true Christianity is for failures. People who screw up and know it. People who embrace grace at the risk of abusing it. People who are as shifty and unstable as the sand—and thus need a rock on which to build.

It's for losers.

GOD
OF
RELATIONSHIP

⌐THE SILENCE OF THE SONG⌐
Winn Collier

Tom Conlon is a raw, earthy artist, braver than most of us. Tom has the courage to be silent. I first heard of Tom Conlon when we moved to Clemson, South Carolina. He is a legend here. He has given away his life, his heart, and more CDs than probably even he knows. After hearing frequent mention of this iconic guitarist, I asked, "So, when is he coming back?"

"Nobody knows. He isn't singing right now."

A silent singer. Tom needed time away, solitude, rest, a season listening to the hushed harmonies of God. It requires courage to cease offering what others expect. It requires courage to be silent.

Why must we have something to say? Why must we always explain God or offer a hasty response to even the most reflective questions? Why are we so comfortable with noise? Why do we resist solitude?

It seems we are afraid—afraid of the quiet. In the quiet, the roar of our doubts might overwhelm us. In the solitude, our grip on the imaginary existence we have created and craftily named reality slips. When the noise stills, we find we are addicted. We are addicted to its insidious rhythms, drowning out God's whispered invitation to meet Him in our rawest place: our broken heart, where we connect with our pain, our questions, and our desperation.

To be silent is to be broken. The eagerness to speak sometimes hints of a life that has yet to enter the deeper sorrows, the agony of a world that isn't heaven. Guarding ourselves from these dark corners, we rush forward, running after the reality we created to numb us from ourselves. We find, though, that we are also numbed to the lover of our soul. He invites us to "be still and know" He is God (Psalm 46:10). But we can't risk that. To be still is to be quiet. To be quiet is to hear our heart. To hear our heart is to know all is not well. And that is far too dangerous. Better to simply enjoy the noise.

Tom is again offering the gift of his music. On his new CD, he reflected: "After a year of 'laying low', it's good to be playing music again, though I'm learning that all of it, especially the silence, is a song."

God waits in the quiet. His invitation woos us from the place we call safety ... but isn't. Be brave. Enter the silence. God will meet you there.

EVEN DEEPER
Read Exodus 14:14, Psalm 131, and Isaiah 55:1-2. Is there space for quiet in your life? Carve out at least thirty minutes for it this week.

PRAYER
God of silent whispers, please quiet my heart, quiet my life. I want to be pulled from addiction to noise. I want to be pulled deeper into You.

⁓THE RIGHT TOOL⁓
Lynn Hickernell

I'm smart enough to realize certain tools are made for doing specific tasks and not others. I've never tried to nail a screw into the wall with a hammer, or play a CD on a turntable. Only one key on my key ring starts my car, and only one unlocks my front door. For some jobs, only the right tool will work.

In the account of Jesus healing the boy in Mark 9:14-29, the disciples try on their own to heal the boy. They fail. When they ask Jesus why, Christ explains some things require prayer and fasting. In other words, some jobs require using the tool of submission: turning control over to God.

God provides us with many tools, such as intellect, energy, and skills, which we may mistake as our private resources—all we need to manage life. However, these tools are imperfect when in our control. As this story reminds us, our tools are limited. We need God.

Like the boy in need, we are afflicted with trials that can only be alleviated through prayer. Many of our struggles would see relief if we would, like the disciples, recognize our weakness and come to God for help.

Perhaps we believe our predicaments do not merit His attention, and mistakenly believe we should keep them to ourselves. Maybe we fall too easily into culture's trap of relying solely on the individual and rejecting the hand another offers. We often insist on using all the tools at our disposal before we admit our utter weakness. When our resources are exhausted, we are forced to turn to God.

How much better if we could run to God at the outset rather than trying to solve my problems with our own broken tools? Why can't we, as the old hymn advocates, "carry everything to God in prayer"?

We must admit our constant need for God. We must join with the honest prayer of David: "I pour out my complaint before him; before him I tell my trouble. When my spirit grows faint within me, it is you who know my way. In the path where I walk men have hidden a snare for me" (Psalm 142: 2-3).

EVEN DEEPER
Read Romans 6:13. What is your "go to" tool? Your humor, intellect, or power? Take that tool out. Ask God what you should do with it.

PRAYER
God, I am troubled. I am overwhelmed. God, only You know what I should do. Only You can meet the need I face. I lay it in Your hands.

⬷ OBEDIENCE ⬵
Margaret Feinberg

The word is four simple letters and can be echoed in one syllable. It's a word we've been trained by since we were children. At times, it still makes us wince.

Obey.

It looks harmless at first glance. Almost lonely as it sits there. It causes the Pharisee to exclaim and the backslider to pout. It divides those who build on the sand and those who construct on the rock. The wise and the foolish part over it, and those who are faithful know its cost. Once the service ends and pews return to their empty state, this small word determines the character of the believer.

Obey. Pause. Quiet your mind. Reflect. Is there anything God has asked you to do that you're not doing?

Maybe it's something big. A calling. You're supposed to be in seminary. You were supposed to take that job even though it didn't pay as well. Or maybe it's something little. You were asked to fast. You should have called your aunt two days ago. God asked you to step away from a habit.

Whatever it is, God has not forgotten. And in His grace, He hasn't allowed you to forget either. He loves you, and more than your spiritual activity, He's looking for obedience. He wants to give you more, entrust you with greater things. He wants to funnel more of His blessing, strength, and light through you. But that one small point of disobedience has limited the flow. Maybe you hadn't noticed. But He has. And that's why He's taken this time to remind you. To give you another chance. To encourage you to move. Make that step.

Obey.

He never said it would be easy. He never said it would be fun. He never said it wouldn't require strength, courage, and your will. He simply said, "Obey."

"But the man who looks intently into the perfect law that gives freedom, and continues to do this, not forgetting what he has heard, but doing it—he will be blessed in what he does" (James 1:25).

EVEN DEEPER
Read 1 Samuel 15:21-23. Can you think of an area of disobedience in your own life? What can you do to change? Do it.

PRAYER
Father, forgive me for not responding to Your commands. Forgive me for looking the other way, finding other things to do with my time, and trying to convince myself that You really hadn't spoken to me. I choose to obey You. I love You.

⮜IN SEARCH OF⮞
Tom Mulnix

Contentment. That seemingly unattainable feeling that plagues each one of us. We've all tasted contentment, but have you noticed its brevity?

Consider the infant. After feeding, a dry diaper, and being rocked in loving arms, blissful sleep comes easily. But it will be short-lived.

A kid longing for the latest toy on the market will be satisfied with having it until the next craze hits the shelf. So goes the search for contentment.

This feeling that something is missing plagues us all. It may be as basic as hunger, or as complex as issues of the heart, but every day, each of us conducts a flurry of activity searching to fill the void. It doesn't help that the world is constantly telling (and selling) us that we must have, look like, or experience the latest hype.

It's been this way since the fall of man. Only when God walked with Adam in the Garden did man feel true contentment. And we've been in search of it ever since.

In John chapter four, a Samaritan woman went to a well to draw water. Jesus met her there, and it is revealed that the woman had been married five times and was currently with a sixth man. Jesus said, "Everyone who drinks this water will be thirsty again, but whoever drinks the water I give him will never thirst." Later, Jesus offered an invitation, "If anyone is thirsty, let him come to me and drink" (John 7:37).

Jesus offers us the same. We don't have to be thirsty. We are on a quest for contentment. Whether it is the climb up the corporate ladder or an addiction, we are searching for satisfaction.

Author Max Lucado wrote, "We are bound together by broken dreams and collapsed promises. Fortunes that were never made, families that were never built, promises that were never kept. We're thirsty for a clean conscience, we crave a clean slate, we yearn for a fresh start."

Jesus offers water that will forever satisfy our thirst. His well is a place where our search can end.

EVEN DEEPER
Consider John 7:38. What are the things in your life that are leaving you feeling unsatisfied? Take them to the well of Christ.

PRAYER
I'm tired. I'm lonely. I'm thirsty. Jesus, I want to drink from the well that never runs dry. Fill me with Your peace.

HOLDING GOD'S HAND
Margaret Feinberg

In a single generation, the entire script of life has been rewritten. You can call it postmodernism. You can call it the evolution of the metanarrative. Or you can just call it what the rest of us do: real life. The patterns worn by our parents have eroded, and we are left to sketch our own designs into this precious lifespan. In other words, our lives just don't look like those of our parents. We run on a clock with slower hands. We're getting married, developing careers and finding our niches later in life.

Young adults generally consider at least one area of their lives completely together—whether it's marriage, relationships, or career—but consider other areas in a constant state of uncertainty. As a result, we are self-proclaimed late bloomers in some regard. We may not have discovered "the one." We may not know what we want to do with our lives. We may still be searching for our niche, a sense of community, a place to lay down roots.

While the scenarios of our lives differ in some regards—location, job title, support network—the core human experience is the same. We share a common bond in the basic challenges we face: responding to adversity, waiting for God's best, handling the rejections of life. Without a road map, many of us are pioneering our own way.

Though we look upon the future with hope, we have no idea what's around the next corner. So we are left dependent on the Creator. The choice is ours: Will we choose to hold His hand?

It may be the biggest decision we will ever make, and it's one we must continually remake. Will we choose to hold His hand through triumph and tragedy? Will we choose to hold His hand during the surprises and curve balls life throws our way?

Holding His hand through life will alter our perspective and influence our responses. It will challenge us not to settle for second best. It will remind us that those who continue to abide in the vine will eventually produce fruit. It will awaken us to the reality that this life, as challenging as it may be at times, is still a wonderful and precious gift.

Whose hand are you holding?

EVEN DEEPER
Read Psalm 37:23-24 and James 4:8. Reflect on your schedule. Who are you more dependent upon in the daily rigors of life? Yourself or God? What can you do to make yourself more dependent on Him?

PRAYER
Father, I need your presence in my life in greater measures. Too often I choose to walk this path alone. Forgive me. Embrace me. Take my hand, Let's travel through life together.

⌐WARM EMBRACE⌐
Margaret Feinberg

Father, why do we exchange our citizenship for a work permit? Instead of crawling up on Your lap, why do we run to the fields? Rather than walk into Your presence, why do we try to earn Your favor?

The child inside us cries out. But our grown-up side says, "Hush. Don't bother the Father now. He has many other children with more severe problems than you."

Then the adversary steps in: "You only come when you have problems. You haven't done anything for Him. So don't bother coming at all." And the wheels begin to spin. The hands begin to toil. Sweat beads roll.

Prayer. Intercession. Worship. Bible study. Memorization. Service. Offerings.

And slowly the bag of religious tricks weighs less and less. Until it is empty, and so are we. But Father never demanded a bag of anything.

Only us.

    Empty.

        Naked.

            Broken.

                Desperate.

                    In need.

He invites us into His kingdom. He invites us into His throne room. He invites us to the banquet table.

The dress? A commoner's clothes. A cloak of humility. These are the proper garments for entrance to the King's inner chambers.

The invitation seems to welcome the poor and empty-handed. The warm embrace of the King confirms it, and reminds us that we should have come long ago.

DEEPER WALK
Read Matthew 19:13-15. Reflect on what prevents you from running to God. Ask God to remove those things from your life. Center your heart on God as Father. Imagine His warm embrace.

PRAYER
Father, I want to know You more intimately. I long for Your embrace. Help me to draw nearer to You every day.

⸎GOODBYE⸎
Zachry O. Kincaid

Our son is approaching two years old, and already he is a great theologian. In fact, he may know almost all he needs to know. Yesterday, as I made a last ditch effort not to forget anything on my way to work, dodging past truck and tricycle to reach the door, he said with waving gesture and careless smile, "Bye … bye … dad-dee."

It was in my car that morning that "bye, bye, daddy" overwhelmed me. "He almost knows it all," I said to myself. He knows sin and need. I passed it on to him as my father passed it on to me. It has been passed down the crooked line all the way from the day that started this business of decline, a day where creature became creator, a title stolen through vying for rights to hand-held fruit (of all things).

My son knows goodbye. My heart aches heavy for a shelter that will protect him from goodbyes, but it was ransacked with the close of Eden's doors. There is no shelter. Now, found wandering, we dread departures for they are the preliminaries to funerals. Life has boundaries that are only erased with the first glimpse of eternity, the fairyland where goodbyes are hushed by welcomes that have no aches.

He knows goodbye, and not even the dawning of new technology can lighten this load. I hope our son's knowledge of goodbye will cast only temporary shadows and that understanding might lead to wisdom that takes root in Him who shouted, "Hello!" from His perch of ascending clouds some time ago. This hello still frightens man-made suns with their Babel fists raised in ignorance. May my son always welcome as a friend He who is the shelter, a true lamp that guides feet and gives light to paths.

EVEN DEEPER

Today, notice the number of times you say "goodbye," and may it cause you to notice further how time really has an end. Find comfort in Revelation 21:4.

PRAYER

God, I often think mortality is for everyone else. Teach me to rightly count my days and to use this particular day for your purposes and not my own.

HEARD ABOVE THE DIN
Eric Hurtgen

It's the twenty-first century, and we live ceiling-to-floor, wall-to-wall encased in noise. Noise emanates from our television sets and our florescent lights, ambulances, police cars, and car stereos, rattling the ground for blocks. This noise is distracting, grabbing our attention with images on our computers, graffiti on highway overpasses, and five-story movie screens.

Somehow, this noise is comforting as well, the rattle of the train in the distance, the screech of brakes, and voices down the hallway. It dissolves the fear and aching loneliness. We're connected, yet disconnected. We search for our own voice, fighting to be heard amid the many other voices.

But what happens when we are still? Do we long for more voices and noise? Or do we surrender to the one whose voice comes as a whisper, quiet enough to be missed amid the buzz and hum? Does this voice only come to us when we are still, when we have turned away from the din? It's hard for us to know, trapped as we are amid too much commotion. Even our gas station pumps have voices now. We don't get away from the clamor easily.

What would happen if we were still? Where would we be without the voices telling us what to buy, who to be, where to go? When we have been still, we have suffered awkward silence. But it is only in the silence that Wisdom whispers to us. And it is only when we are silent that we are truly able to hear.

To listen for the voice of wisdom, we must put ourselves in a place to hear Him. To do this, we must turn away from the competing voices. We must be silent before Him and wait. It is no accident that Jesus instructs us to go to our closets to speak to the Father. It is no accident that we are instructed to speak few words. He knows how much we need to hear His voice over the din. Let us learn to be still and how to be in the quiet. There, we can make a place to hear His voice.

EVEN DEEPER

Meditate on Matthew 6:5-14. Make The Lord's Prayer your prayer, and find a quiet place alone where you can pray through your prayer, giving the Lord ample room to speak.

PRAYER

Quiet my soul within me, Lord. Let my heart be stirred only by You now. I will wait for Your kingdom, and listen for Your voice.

One night, my wife and I were on our way to meet some friends when she mentioned in passing a rumor that Lauryn Hill was playing a secret show at a club nearby. Not to let such a treat pass us by, I bee-lined it for the club in question.

For those of you living under a rock, Lauryn Hill is the ex-Fugee member whose solo album, *The Miseducation Of Lauryn Hill*, sold fourteen million copies and cleaned up at the Grammys a couple of years back. Her music is soulful and bold — and her message is overtly Christian.

The concert was truly a once-in-a-lifetime event. There she was, fifteen feet in front of us, alone on a stage with nothing but a stool and her acoustic guitar. The music was awe-inspiring. She began the concert by telling the crowd she chose to have no accompaniment because she wanted us to listen to the lyrics. Listen to what the songs were saying. Truly get them.

And they didn't disappoint. The spiritual bent of her previous work pales in comparison to what we heard that night. Every song had blatantly Christ-centered content. From "Jerusalem," which was nothing but beautifully interwoven Scripture, to songs sung from God to His children, to songs about righteousness, the river of God and freedom in Christ ... on and on they went. "The road to Hell is paved with good intentions," began the first song of the night. To answer her critics: "They don't know me, if they don't know my Father."

I heard more truth in that club than I have in many churches. That night I saw in living color what it means to be light in the darkness. That night I stood within earshot of someone I deeply respect and admire, someone who will touch millions of lives through uncompromised lyrics and amazing music. She will give answers to people asking, "God, where are you?" She will point people to a relationship with Christ.

Yet, the Church won't acknowledge her. She's "secular," and her music isn't sold in Christian bookstores.

When I read *WALK ON: The Spiritual Journey of U2* (Relevant Books), I have to tell you, I saw Bono—and the Church—in a completely different light. The book details the story of a man, and a band, that came out of the fires of spiritual renewal in Dublin. In the formative years of the band's existence, Bono, the Edge and Larry were unashamed, Spirit-filled Christians. They attended the Shalom Fellowship in Dublin faithfully, and they talked constantly about God in their music and in the media.

Then, after their debut album, *Boy*, and the growing fame that came with it, their church told the boys that the Lord wanted them to disband the group. They were forced to choose between the wishes of their sincere, yet misguided, congregation, and the passion God put in their hearts to make music that would change the world. They chose the latter, and their church shunned them.

The book then goes into the story of U2's music and career, how the three have never wavered in their faith in God and their love for Him, but did grow to reject legalistic religion. (Good for them.)

As much spiritual impact as U2 has had on the world over the last twenty years—from raising billions of dollars for the world's poor to pointing people to Christ through their lyrics—imagine how much more impact they would have had if their church had chosen to embrace them instead of reject them. Imagine if they had had a spiritual umbrella to support and guide them through their journey, rather than being thrown out to find their own way in a life of unsheltered fame. Imagine if the Church supported them rather than criticized them. Imagine.

The question is pertinent because the Shalom Fellowship is not unlike many American churches. Where would Creed be if Lee University had not expelled lead singer Scott Stapp when they caught him smoking weed as a student there? What if they would have helped him get his heart and life straight instead of slamming the door behind him? Creed has sold something like twelve million albums over the last few years. In their music, they are crying out for God, but they don't know where to find Him because the Church has said, "We don't want you."

I think artists like Lauryn Hill, Lifehouse, Creed, U2— all who started in the Church and are at the top of the charts—need the Church to stand up and support them. If we're ever going to get outside of our bubble and impact culture, we need to stand with, support and embrace the voices out there that love God—or are looking for God—and just happen to be outside of our comfort zones of familiarity. Imagine if for the last twenty years Bono was getting fed at the Shalom Fellowship, what a difference it would have made in the lives of millions of people. Imagine Lauryn Hill with the Church standing by her side. She's bringing the only Christian message most of her fans will ever really pay attention to. You think most of the people at that club with me at 1 A.M. were in church that Sunday?

No, these artists aren't perfect, but in their own ways they're pointing millions of people to the Lord. They're impacting lives and affecting culture more than the preachers on TBN ever could. They're out there in the trenches, on a journey to find a relationship with their Creator, and they're bringing an entire radio-listening and video-watching generation with them in their quest. I say it's time the Church wakes up and gets out there. It's time the light stops shining upon itself and starts to make a difference in the darkness, because that's where it's needed most. That's where these artists are. That's where the real mission field is. And I think that's where Jesus would be, too.

⌒RIGHT OR RIGHTEOUS?⌒
Margaret Feinberg

The Sermon on the Mount is a dividing message. It makes you either want to climb the mount of faith or run from it. Christ's words outline just how difficult the journey can become. Guard your personal relationships. Give with abandon. Forgive. Forgive. And then, forgive some more.

One of the greatest challenges is the command to love your enemies. Note that Jesus didn't say enemy, but enemies. He must have known there would be many and that they would take all different forms. Neighbors. Relatives. Spouses. Children. Bosses. And rather than live overseas, they tend to live next door or inside your own home. Yet Jesus' challenge is the same: "Love your enemies and pray for those who persecute you" (Matthew 5:43-48).

It's backward thinking. Embrace those who hurt others. Love those who hate. Yet in the kingdom of God, it makes sense. Jesus goes on to explain why: "In order that you may be sons of your Father who is in heaven."

That kind of forgiveness and love—it makes us His. It seems to make no sense, but it makes us His as our identity is shifted from this world into the next. It challenges us to make decisions based on eternity rather than on the temporal.

Fortunately, Christ didn't just preach this love, He lived it. A few chapters later we find Him hanging mangled on the cross. Pierced. Beaten. Robbed of His own clothes. Bloodstained. Pain-inflicted. It's in this state that He cries out not against them, but for them, "Father, forgive them, for they do not know what they are doing."

If He wanted to be right, He could have reminded them of the coming judgment or invoked one of His own. But instead He chose to be righteous and live out the very commandment He had spoken.

It's precisely in those points we're wronged, those moments we partake of the cross, when we have no obligation, when it's not comfortable, that Christ quietly gives us the opportunity to become more like Him. Maybe it's a bill you don't have any obligation to pay. Maybe it's a workplace problem you have no reason to overlook. Maybe it's a person who only knows how to wrong you in words or action. Maybe it's not what's been done, but what's been left undone. Whatever the reason, whatever the source, the invitation remains—to be right or to be righteous.

DEEPER WALK
Consider Matthew 6:14, 18:21-22. How can you respond in righteousness when you've been wronged?

PRAYER
Father, increase my level of faith and grace. Help me to choose to love my enemies and reflect your Son.

◆DON'T BE A SQUARE◆
Tom Mulnix

Have you ever seen a square watermelon? Recently farmers in Japan introduced square watermelons to the fruit-buying public. Some twenty years ago, a farmer from Zentsuji came up with the idea of making a cube-shaped watermelon, solving several inherent problems of traditionally shaped watermelons. One common problem was storage, the difficulty encountered in fitting large, round watermelons in the refrigerator. They're also hard to slice when they're rolling all over the place. The farmer achieved his cubed results by growing the melons in glass boxes. The fruit simply assumed the same shape.

In Romans 12:2, Paul instructed us not to "conform any longer to the pattern of this world." It's a struggle. Do you ever feel there is a glass cube pressing around your life? From birth, we're set on a course to ensure we'll fit right into the masses. Rows of cookie cutter houses, everyone working nine-to-five jobs to pay for things the media say we need.

Take a closer look at yourself. God made each of us with unique characteristics, abilities, dreams, and aspirations. Are you following those dreams and using those abilities, or have you been squeezed into a glass mold that society has hoisted on you? We have been told that our desires should be practical, the longing of our hearts are ridiculous. We are tempted to conform. But it was the Creator who placed in each of us a passion. He didn't place it there for it to be denied. But as long as we continue to take our cues from culture, we won't explore. We won't follow our design.

EVEN DEEPER
Take stock of your God-given passions. Ask yourself, "What would I be doing if I knew I couldn't fail?" Read Psalm 139:1-6. Think about your answer in light of the verses you read.

PRAYER
Thank You, Lord, for ordering every step of my life. Help me to step into my passion and become the person You created me to be.

❧STRAIGHT AHEAD❧
Pat Matuszak

"Tough shot," I said, watching Pete's Titleist hook out over Lake Michigan like a trick Frisbee throw. "At least you won't do that again today."

"Oh yeah, watch this," he smirked.

Pete stepped up to the tee again, repeating the exact same shot. I'd never seen him shank like that on any hole until the dreaded number six. "This is like the Bermuda Triangle," he moaned. "Every time I play here the same thing happens." He trudged down the fairway and dropped a ball at the edge of the grass where his first two had veered to their watery graves. The rest of the afternoon, none of his shots hooked, and his game returned to normal.

It reminded me of something I learned in driver's ed about steering a car. If I focused on what I was trying to avoid, the car would inevitably veer toward it. Somehow my intention to avoid the thing I feared caused me to drift towards it. Our teacher would cue us to look ahead by saying "Horizon. Eyes on the horizon." He trained us to look out, farther than the problem area, and visually grab a focal point in the road ahead. Instead of concentrating on where we didn't want to go, we zeroed in on where wanted to end up.

Sometimes what we are trying to avoid propels toward us

like a magnet. As we focus on avoidance, it sucks up our resources. Our intention not to do the wrong thing draws so much energy that we don't have any left to invest in doing the right thing.

In Luke 9:62, Jesus explained how the diligent farmer puts his hands on the plow and doesn't look back. He marks a line ahead, keeping his eyes on it as he carves straight furrows through the fresh soil. If the farmer looks back or off to the side, he veers off course. Jesus' solution was similar to my driving instructor's: Look ahead. Don't look back. Focus on your destination and lesser worries won't sidetrack your efforts.

EVEN DEEPER
Read Philippians 3:13-14. As you drive today, spend the time reflecting on God's parable of focus. Is there any area of your life where you are tempted to look back? As your mind veers off track, switch your thoughts and prayer efforts to things you know God wants you to embrace. Set a focal point this week for your action and prayer.

PRAYER
God, I am tempted to look back, veer to the side, wander around, and get completely off track. Pull me into Your strong grip. I want to move straight ahead for Your glory.

TANDEM JUMP
Laura Elliott

I jumped out of a plane today. I did what they call a tandem jump. I was harnessed to a certified instructor, and together, we made the jump.

I did this insane thing for two reasons: I have always wanted to skydive. And it was a stretch for me. It is out of my comfort zone to not know what I am doing and to completely trust someone else (in this case with my life). It was a spiritual experience.

On the climb to 10,000 feet, I was reviewing what I was supposed to do. It was relatively simple. I was to listen to my instructor as we positioned ourselves on the wing. I was to cross my arms when we jumped and then put my body in an arch as soon as possible. I was not to grab my instructor's hands, and I was to do whatever he told me to do on the way down. But most importantly, I was to have fun and enjoy the ride.

As the crop plane approached the jump point, I continued my review and began to see a parallel to a spiritual truth. What was I being asked to do? Pack a parachute, fly the plane? No, I was to trust in the instructor, the pilot, the plane, and the parachute packer. My knowledge was limited. I didn't know how it all worked, nor was I asked to learn. My task was simple: trust, obey. I was not asked to do anything other than trust in the ones who had it under control.

God is attuned to our journey, and He has it under control. God will do everything necessary to see that we land where He has designed. God is the pilot, and we are simply along for the ride.

Our concerns should be relatively few. Trust in the goodness of God. Don't worry about all God is responsible for. Enter the spiritual community God has created for us. Obey Him when He speaks. Enjoy the ride.

EVEN DEEPER
Read Matthew 6:25-34. Do a word study on "trust" in the Psalms. As you read, is there something that comes to your mind, some area where you are not resting in the strong arms of God? Close your eyes. Give it to Him. Jump!

PRAYER
Strong and steady God, why do I worry about the things only You can handle—especially when You have promised that You will? Teach me to trust. Teach me to jump.

⌐NAME BUILDER⌐
J.R. Rushik

Then they said, "Come, let us build ourselves a city, with a tower that reaches to the heavens, so that we may make a name for ourselves and not be scattered over the face of the whole earth" (Genesis 11:4).

"I will make you into a great nation and I will bless you; I will make your name great, and you will be a blessing" (Genesis 12:2).

These two stories in the Bible stand in stark contrast. The first is the building of the tower of Babel, and the second is the blessing of Abraham. Although they are only separated in the text by one chapter, they are polar opposites in their approaches to living.

In the first story, the people of Babel decided to build a large tower, a work of art that would forever immortalize and symbolize their great power and knowledge. Their goal was to "make a name for themselves." The result was the eventual destruction of not only their edifice but also their identity. The tower was destroyed, and the people were scattered throughout the earth.

Abraham took a different road. God called him to take a journey of faith, and he responded with obedience. He was eager for his name to reflect God's covenant purposes on the earth. The overflow of his obedience was a dramatic blessing from God. God promised to make

Abraham the father of a great nation with a name that would forever be known as "great."

The people of Babel tried to "make" their name. They were scattered.

Abraham acted with simple obedience. His name is great even today, a father of nations.

Someone once said, "We should take care of the depth, God will take care of the breadth." Efforts focused on building ourselves will profit little, but energy focused on deepening our relationship with God will produce lasting results.

EVEN DEEPER
Study 2 Peter 1:4-11. Perform a random, anonymous act of kindness. This unnamed act will help reinforce the call to live a humble, obedient life.

PRAYER
Lord, enable me to be obedient to the calling You have placed on me. I trust Your faithfulness.

⌒A PERILOUS SAFETY⌒
Winn Collier

Sometimes a firm footing on solid dirt poses a graver
risk than a wild-eyed leap over the edge. A blind jump
off a six-hundred-foot high locomotive bridge is an
absurd risk —unless the Midnight Special barrels toward
you. Your perception of risk adjusts in moments like
these. Dark. Shrill whistle. Desperate. Lights blinding.
Alone. Nothing below. Train thunders. Tracks roar. Leap.

It's human nature to play it safe. We don't ask the girl
out until we get the proper signals. We don't leave the
job we despise until the next one is in the bag. Even in
Vegas with the adrenaline rush of a high-stakes gamble,
the game is to pick the table you think offers the best
odds for lady luck to roll your direction. They call it
playing the odds—the alluring quest to minimize risk.
We are a tribe of safe-dwellers. We display a frequent
aversion to risk.

God doesn't. In fact, He rarely asks anything of us that
doesn't demand risk. Consider Abraham. God's plan was
daring, simple, and woefully short on information.
Abraham was called simply to pack up and leave. No
map. No travel brochures of intriguing sites along the
journey. No cloud to guide the way. Just go.

Abraham had a choice. He could sit, comfortable and
content, enjoying peaceful days with familiar sunsets—
potential boredom but certainly safe. Or he could follow
the deep soul stirring to run after God, a daring plunge

into faith. Dangerous. Definitely *not* safe. *But* absolutely a life lived full on, drawn to more than a mere snug, amiable existence.

A paradox lurks in these moments of choice. What we believe is safe often really isn't. If safety is only "freedom from physical harm," a timid refusal to God's adventure makes sense. But what if, rather than guarding our temporary comforts, ultimate safety demands our faint, mortal hearts be captured by the purposes of God? If accurate, then lounging on the shore—a respectable distance from the torrential gale—might be the most treacherous place of all. It is a perilous safety.

So God asks us to risk. To move. We must choose. But we hesitate, uncertain. We don't know where it leads. It is a fearful place—not knowing. As Marilyn Ferguson said, "It's not so much that we're afraid of change or so in love with the old ways, but it's the place in between that we fear ... It's like being between trapezes. It's Linus when his blanket is in the dryer. There's nothing to hold on to."

Leap. Hold on to God. Anything else is a perilous safety.

EVEN DEEPER
Read 2 Samuel 22. Take a risk this week. Confront that fear that has nagged you.

PRAYER
God of danger, teach me to leap ... straight into Your arms.

⚘SOUND⚘
Zachry O. Kincaid

Sound. Do you hear it? Not the useless loud noise, but sound that is voice-made-praise. Do you hear the rustle of the wind that gives song to the trees? Do you hear the cricket's summer chorus or the sparrow's humble chatter? Do you hear the collision of the rain with the ground, or the slow rippling water as the evening sun melts into it? Do you hear the conversation of geese overhead, the distant bark of a dog at dusk, or the buzzing of a bee as it dances beside a flower one windy day?

I wonder if God hears these things. He must. And I wonder if it is our lack of praise that causes them to reach His ears, filling in where we have grossly neglected voicing praise to our Creator.

We believe our life is better filled with noise, with the wail of phones and the exhausting hurry of our exhaust. We are the creators of busyness and medicated necessities, the havoc that allows time to define our day instead of our day defining time. It is this belief that reduces our voice to mere noise and empowers birds and trees and insects and dogs to raise their extra volume of praise to our Father.

King David was a man who heard the sound. One of the busiest men alive during his day—with the joint responsibilities of leading a nation, caring for a family, and conquering other peoples—he still found time to stop and listen and sing back to God. David penned more than seventy psalms (the word psalm itself means to celebrate the praises of God in song). David saw God's chariot in the clouds and a garment for the earth in the sea. He perceived poetry in God's hand feeding all the creatures on earth. He paused long enough to hear the earth chanting God's qualities—His enduring faithfulness, provision, forgiveness, protection, guidance, and most of all, His unfailing love.

I'm sure not all the psalms David wrote flowed fluidly and effortlessly from his pen. He had to experience times when he was tempted to allow the demands of a kingdom to drown out the reverberating sound of God's goodness. Yet David continued to slice out moments in his day to listen and to make a joyful noise right back. He wasn't about to let the trees and birds outdo him.

Will you?

EVEN DEEPER
Meditate on Psalm 104, then read about Jesus' triumphal entry in Luke 19:28-40. Go someplace quiet. Sit there for thirty minutes.

PRAYER
Your world is full of chatter that brings life to my ears. As I hear the morning birds, attune my ears to hear Your words through the love of a neighbor, through Scripture, through song, through creation.

⌘A HOLY TASTING⌘
Winn Collier

Recently I have explored the discipline of Lectio Divina, an ancient devotional practice that emerged in the early days of the church and was nurtured along the centuries by the Benedictine movement. Lectio Divina is Latin for *holy reading*, and it offers an invitation to hear the voice of God arise out of the Scriptures.

Steeped in technical, literal—almost scientific— exegesis of Scripture, it can be difficult to move past analyzing God's Word and deeper into the unhurried art of listening to it. Lectio Divina is not antithetical to sound interpretation of the text's meaning, but it does challenge the sad reality that technical interpretation can often become our god. We seize God's words, but we miss God's heart.

Quieting our mind, engaging our spirit, being moved by more than sentence structure and original meanings— why are these simple-sounding notions so rare to experience? Why is connecting our heart with God's such a struggle?

Could it be due to our loss of the art of savoring, our loss of the pleasure of taste? Listening to God's heart belongs to the realm of beauty—the world of experience, image, and taste. We often live in the realm of science— the world of exactness, logic, and duty.

We are a people of solutions. Give us a problem, and we'll fix it. Offer a question, and we'll find an answer.

We are an efficient, self-achieving, driven band. There is little room for ambiguity, little space for pondering, and only rare moments to pause, breathe deeply, and wonder if there could be more to our restless wanderings than a slavish quest for the holy grail—getting it right. Unfortunately, getting it right plays no part in experiencing beauty.

In the heart-tugging movie, *Kate and Leopold*, Leopold is a royal duke transplanted through a time portal from 1876 into the present. The quirky plot is the budding romance between a successful modern woman and … well … a duke from 1876. Far more interesting than the main storyline, however, is the sub-plot: Leopold's attempts to come to terms with life in the modern age. The world he left has vanished, and he isn't certain he likes what is in its place. In one poignant scene, Leopold's frustrated observation is telling: "Life is not solely composed of tasks, but tastes." And he is right.

If our heart has chilled, the voice of God grown distant, perhaps we need space to savor. The psalmist knew this and offered this invitation: "Taste and see that the Lord is good" (Psalm 34:8).

EVEN DEEPER
Meditate on Psalm 63. Savor God. Enjoy a sunset. Take a walk in the woods.

PRAYER
Beautiful One, help me to taste You, to breathe You.

⌒SEEING GRACE⌒
Faith Hopler

Grace is like the tree growing in the center of the house of faith: often walked around, talked around, built around, but never examined very closely. This attribute of God holds us up; without it we would collapse. We use the word flippantly; it's the coin of the Kingdom. But what is grace? We see its astounding effect in the very possibility of a relationship with God. But what is at the heart of grace itself? When I attempt to answer this question, a memory comes to mind.

The memory is of sneaking out of bed as a four year old. Bedtime was a power game I played against my parents. I wielded the usual bag of tricks: the bathroom, a glass of water, sudden insomnia. Once these failed, and after my younger brother was asleep in the bunk below, I'd move with commando care to my door and crack it. If the hallway was clear, I'd hide behind the couch, listening to my parents talk. Sometimes I'd hear my parents' firm tread down the hall, and I'd fling myself back into bed— feigning innocent sleep. The thrill of the game was to not get caught, to get away with something without my parents knowing.

One summer night I stole out of bed, restless. I crept across the room and slowly cracked the door. I froze. My mother was standing with her hand on the doorknob. I was caught! But she looked down at me and said, "I was just coming to get you up!" She took my hand, and we went out in our pajamas and bare feet to our tiny front stoop. We ate raisins out of a bowl while the moon rose, and we pointed out the stars poking through the sky. I don't remember what we talked about, but I remember the sliver of light under my door, the shadows in the hall, and the cotton breeze of a summer night winding the shawl of grace tightly around my mother and me. I could scarcely think for happiness.

My poignant memory is of my mother simply wanting to spend time with me, her willfully disobedient little girl. In such a way, the grace of God comes to us as we stand—caught like a child—pushing the limits of His forbearance. He simply says, "Do you want to sit with Me? I'll show you beautiful things."

EVEN DEEPER
As you were reading, did some area of willful rebellion come to mind? Tonight, sit on the steps of your porch, enjoying the grace of God's beauty and releasing whatever you are holding back. Remember Genesis 3:8-10.

PRAYER
Father, I am tired of sneaking away, trying to get by with something. I want to be tucked in tightly to Your grace.

⌐DISCIPLE-MAKING SANDWICH⌐
J.R. Rushik

"All authority in heaven and on earth has been given to me. Therefore go and make disciples of all nations, baptizing them in the name of the Father and of the Son and of the Holy Spirit, and teaching them to obey everything I have commanded you. And surely I am with you always, to the very end of the age" (Matthew 28:19-20).

Trying to fill the Great Commission on our own is like telling a five year old to go in the backyard and make a Corvette with whatever scrap medal he can find. It won't happen. You may get a creative product of his imagination, but you will never get a Corvette. The same is true of those who try to make disciples using their own strength. The task is out of our league, and Jesus knew it. That is why He didn't send us out alone.

The process for "making disciples" is found on both sides of Jesus' instruction, often called the Great Commission. These verses create a disciple-making sandwich, surrounding us with the necessary components to fulfill this calling.

Jesus provided us with the authority to embark on the journey. Our confidence rests in realizing who has commissioned us to go. Jesus said that God has given us "all authority." This is a license to be a disciple-maker. With God's endorsement, the pressure to perform on our own is lifted.

Jesus then offered the comforting phrase, "I am with you always." Jesus doesn't give us authority to make disciples then leave us to flounder on our own. He tells us He will be with us every moment, guiding, instructing, teaching. Jesus is ever-present. Our challenge is to walk in God's nearness. Our responsiveness to the Spirit of God will determine the level to which we are able to connect with His calling.

There are two questions to guide our daily journey: "Am I relying fully on the authority I have in Christ?" And, "Am I allowing Jesus to genuinely 'be with me always'?" These questions point to the two truths wrapped around God's disciple-making charge. The authority of Christ provides license to move ahead while the nearness of Christ offer a strength on which we can lean.

EVEN DEEPER
Read Matthew 9:36-38. Look at your relationships. Is there anyone you are investing your life into, encouraging them to be disciples of Jesus? If not, ask God to bring someone across your path.

PRAYER
God, you offer me an invitation to join your Kingdom, building disciples of you. Help me to see that it is not in my own strength but in yours that I can answer this call.

IF IT AIN'T BROKE, DON'T FIX IT
Allison Foley

This past spring break, my boyfriend and I worked with
Lisa in Boston, cleaning and moving things in her house.
Her apartment held more junk than I had ever seen in
one place. I wanted the place gutted, wiped down from
top to bottom. I was frustrated and even angry because
of all the filth and waste, the disregard for basic sanita-
tion. Her apartment was filled with nasty junk, things
she had absolutely no use for. But that was *my* perspective.

I realized, however, that understanding basic cleanliness
was not the real issue. There was a moment when I
watched Lisa pick up an old dusty backpack off the floor.
She lovingly wiped off the dust and commented that it
belonged to her daughter Rosa, the love of her life. As I
later reflected on the day, the filth, my disgust, and Lisa's
embrace of that backpack, I realized that the clutter in
her apartment was not about *stuff*. All of her strewn
belongings had her heart tied to them. They represented
the few good things she had in this life. Lisa is so scared
of having *nothing* that she hoards *everything*. I realized
my need to be more sensitive, to recognize that these
things represented the hope she had relied on for years.

Isaiah 50:4 says, "The Sovereign Lord has given me an
instructed tongue, to know the word that sustains the
weary." Simply insisting that Lisa clean her house would
not offer a "word to sustain" her. What Lisa needed was

for me to probe her heart and her hurting soul, offering her my own heart of love. Jesus knew that the woman at the well's real need was not the physical water she came to draw, but rather a heart overflowing with the living water only Jesus could supply. What sustaining word do the people around you need?

EVEN DEEPER
Studay Romans 12. Pick one person in your life to pray for this week. Ask God how you can minister to his true needs rather than the needs you have always perceived.

PRAYER
Dear Lord, thank You for the privilege of knowing others to whom we can show Your love. Help me to see the real hurts, the real pain, the real longings of their souls.

AUTHOR INDEX

Jennifer Ashley—*A Spirit of Prostitution, The Dart of Cynicism*

Dan Buck—*Getting Out of the Faith Ghetto*

Winn Collier—*A Holy Tasting, A Modern Day Prodigal, A Perilous Safety, The Silence of the Song*

Kent D. Curry—*Randy's Rules*

Laura Elliott—*Tandem Jump*

Margaret Feinberg—*Escaping the Comparison Trap, Holding God's Hand, Obedience, Warm Embrace, Right or Righteous*

Allison Foley—*If It Ain't Broke, Don't Fix It*

Lynn Hickernell—*The Right Tool*

Faith Hopler—*Forgive These People, Seeing Grace*

Jeremy Hunt—*Who are the Tax Collectors?*

Eric Hurtgen—*Heard above the Din, Whitewashed Tombs*

Zachry O. Kincaid—*Goodbye, Sound*

Jeremy Klaszus—*Christianity Is for Losers*

Robin Lemke—*God is Relevant*

Jessica Leopold—*Wearing God's Pants*

Pat Matuszak—*Straight Ahead*

Tom Mulnix—*Don't Be A Square, In Search Of*

J.R. Rushik—*Name Builder, Disciple-Making Sandwich*

Pick up the other volumes in

Deeper Walk

A Relevant Devotional Series

at

www.RELEVANTSTORE.com

or your local book retailer.

GOD. LIFE. PROGRESSIVE CULTURE.

RELEVANT
magazine

subscribe now and check out the online

version at

RELEVANTMAGAZINE.COM